W9-BLY-819

Fun
Experiments
with
Light

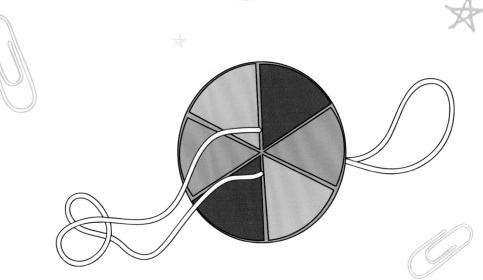

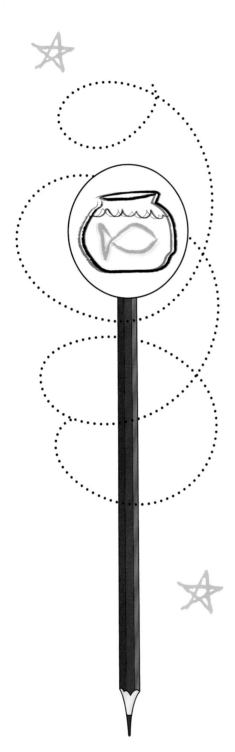

Thanks to the creative team:
Senior Editor: Alice Peebles
Fact checking: Tom Jackson
Design: www.collaborate.agency

Hungry Tomato®
A division of Lerner Publishing Group, Inc.
241 First Avenue North
Minneapolis, MN 55401 USA

For reading levels and more information, look up
this title at www.lernerbooks.com.

Main body text set in Minya Nouvelle Regular 12/15.

The publisher and the author shall not be liable for
any damages allegedly arising from the information
in this book, and they specifically disclaim any liability
from the use or application of any of the contents
of this book. Readers should follow all instructions
and warnings for each experiment in this book and
consult with a parent, teacher, or other adult before
conducting any of the experiments in this book.

Library of Congress Cataloging-in-Publication Data

The Cataloging-in-Publication Data for *Fun Experiments
with Light: Periscopes, Kaleidoscopes, and More* is on file
at the Library of Congress.
ISBN 978-1-5124-3218-3 (lib. bdg.)
ISBN 978-1-5124-4998-3 (EB pdf)

Manufactured in the United States of America
1-41773-23534-4/14/2017

Fun Experiments
with
Light

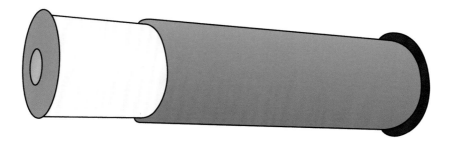

by Rob Ives
Illustrated by Eva Sassin

HUNGRY
TOMATO®
Minneapolis

Safety First

Take care and use good sense with these amazing science experiments—some are very simple, while others are trickier.

Each project includes a list of everything you will need. Most of the items are things you can find around the house, or they are things that are readily available and inexpensive to buy.

Be sure to check out the Amazing Science behind the projects and learn the scientific principles involved in each experiment.

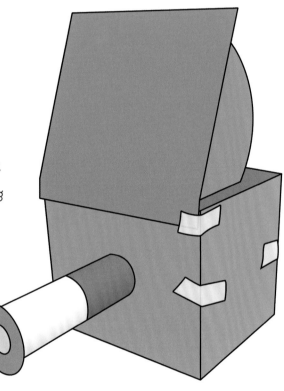

Watch out for this sign throughout the book. You may need help from an adult to complete these tasks.

Contents

Light

Did you know that light is the fastest thing in the universe? In the time it takes you read this sentence, light can travel to the moon and back, in just 2.6 seconds. All light is tiny packets of energy called photons, shot out by atoms. Everything you see is the result of countless tiny photons hitting your eyes! Try out these 12 fun projects to find out a few other things about light too.

You'll see how light is reflected at particular angles when it strikes a mirror. You'll see how light is bent, or refracted, when it passes through glass or water. You'll also see how lenses in telescopes and microscopes use this refraction to magnify things. And there's much more—even seeing a rainbow tells you light is full of color!

You will need:

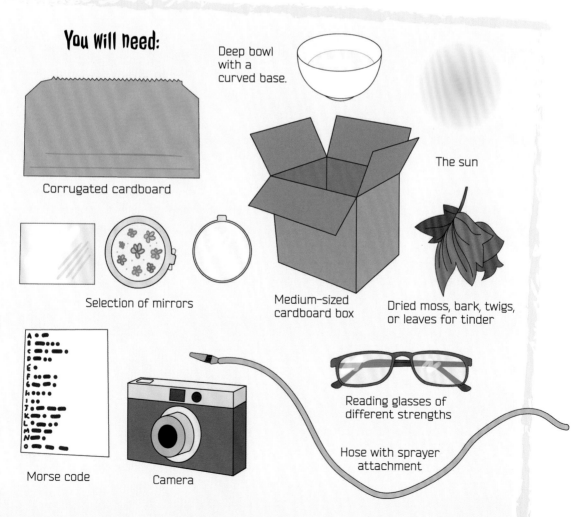

Deep bowl with a curved base.

Corrugated cardboard

The sun

Selection of mirrors

Medium-sized cardboard box

Dried moss, bark, twigs, or leaves for tinder

Reading glasses of different strengths

Hose with sprayer attachment

Morse code

Camera

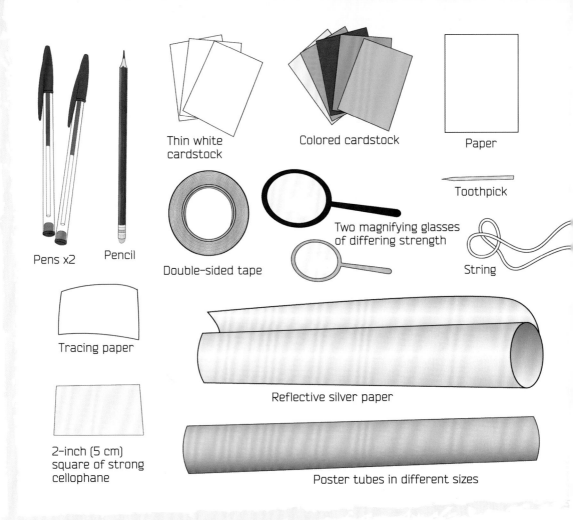

Pens x2

Pencil

Thin white cardstock

Colored cardstock

Paper

Double-sided tape

Two magnifying glasses of differing strength

Toothpick

String

Tracing paper

Reflective silver paper

2-inch (5 cm) square of strong cellophane

Poster tubes in different sizes

What tools will I need?

Utility knife

3.5-inch (90 mm) diameter tape roll

Gaffer tape (or duct tape)

Masking tape

Junior hacksaw

Kitchen Scissors

White glue

Clothespins

Ruler

Periscope

Pencil

Poster tube, 2-inch (50 mm) diameter

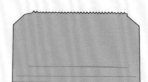

Double-sided tape

Cheap compact mirror with two 2-inch (50 mm) mirrors

A periscope is an optical device for changing your viewpoint. Probably the most famous use for the periscope is in a submarine. It allows the captain to see above the water level without having to break surface and reveal his position. Periscopes also allow small people to see what is going on when they are in the middle of a crowd. They are great for looking over tall walls, and you can even use them for watching TV from behind the sofa!

Tools you will need:
(see page 7)

✭ White glue
✭ Junior hacksaw
✭ Masking tape

Piece of corrugated cardboard

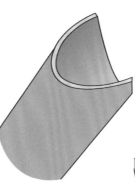

1. Saw the poster tube from the center of one end at a 45-degree angle, on both sides. Have a parent help measure the angle and saw.

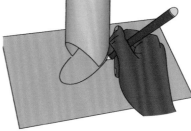

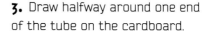

2. Repeat at the other end.

3. Draw halfway around one end of the tube on the cardboard.

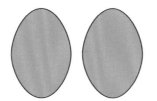

4. Complete the other half of your traced oval shape, then cut it out twice.

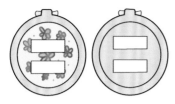

5. Split the mirror in two pieces. Apply double-sided tape to the back of each one.

6. Stick the mirrors to the center of the card ovals

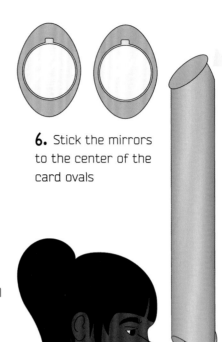

Your periscope is ready to use! Can you see inside that bird's nest in the park?

7. Glue one mirror card to one end and tape it down with masking tape until the glue dries.

8. Repeat at the other end, making sure the mirror is facing the other way. That's it!

Light enters and hits the top mirror.

The top mirror bounces the light onto the mirror below.

The lower mirror shows the view.

Amazing Science

When light hits a mirror at an angle, it bounces off at the same, but opposite, angle. Another mirror facing the first will show the original view. You can also see around corners with your periscope—just hold it sideways!

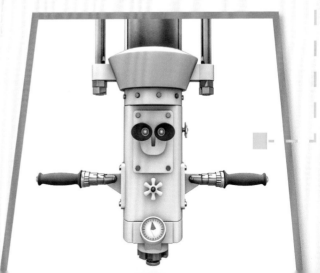

Camera Obscura

The camera obscura was the ancestor of the photographic camera. Here, a lens and a mirror project a picture onto a sheet of tracing paper inside a box. There is also a shade on top to make the image clearer. Many years ago, artists used equipment like this to trace over a projected image. This was a starting point for their painting.

Medium-sized cardboard box

Double sided tape

Tracing paper

A cheap mirror, about 6 x 8 inches (15 x 20 cm)

White cardstock

Cheap reading glasses, +3 minimum strength

Corrugated cardboard

2-inch (50 mm) diameter poster tube

Tools you will need:
(see page 7)

☆ Utility knife
☆ White glue
☆ Clothespins
☆ Masking tape

1. Pop out a lens from the glasses. Cut out a donut shape from corrugated cardboard, 3 inches (75 mm) across with a 1.5-inch (40 mm) diameter hole in the center.

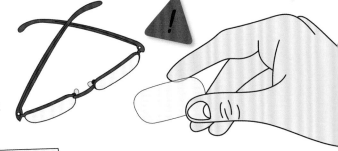

2. Tape the lens over the hole with masking tape.

3. Cut a 4-inch (10 cm) section off the poster tube. Roll up a 8-inch (20 cm) length of white card and make a tube that fits inside the poster tube. The poster tube must be able to move back and forth on the white tube, like a telescope.

4. Glue the end of the poster tube to the lens donut card.

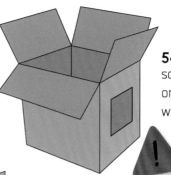

5. Cut a 4-inch square (10 cm) hole in one side of your box with a utility knife.

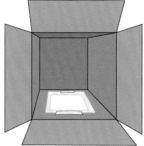

6. Tape the tracing paper over the hole on the inside with masking tape. Make sure it is taut. This is the screen and will be on the top.

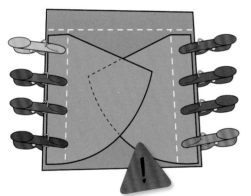

7. Make a shade for the top by cutting three pieces of corrugated cardboard as shown. One is square, the width of the box; and two have a slanted and a curved edge. Allow a 0.5-inch (15 mm) straight margin for each. Glue on the side pieces and hold in place with clothespins as it dries. Glue the square piece along its margin to the box to shade the screen.

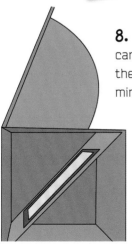

8. Cut out a piece of corrugated cardboard that fits exactly across the diagonal of the box. Fix the mirror to it with double-sided tape.

9. Cut a hole for the lens tube in the front of the box, and fit it in place. Close in the sides and tape them down to finish the camera obscura.

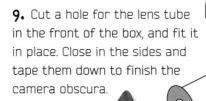

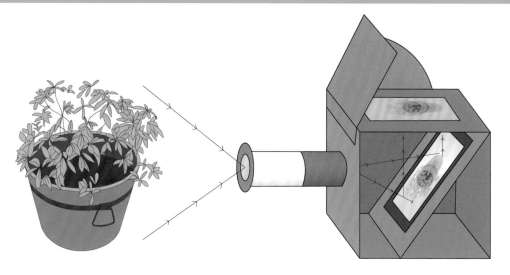

10. Point your lens at a brightly lit scene. Look down at the screen as you move the lens back and forward to focus the image there.

Amazing Science

When a light ray enters glass, it may be bent, or refracted. Lenses have curved surfaces that make all the rays bend towards the same point, or focus. Here, the lens and the mirror focus the light to project the scene onto the tracing paper.

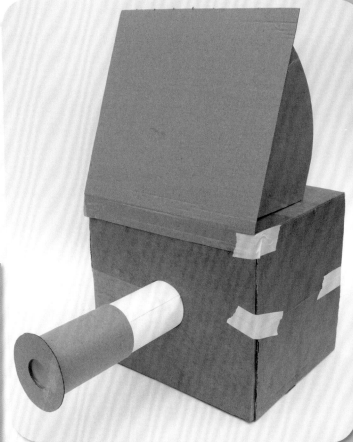

Kaleidoscope

The kaleidoscope is a nineteenth-century invention that uses a tube of three mirrors to create a colorful moving image. The kaleidoscope is so effective at creating swirling, changing colors that kaleidoscopic now means anything with quickly changing, bright colors.

1. Use a utility knife and ruler to cut the tube to roughly 7 inches (180 mm) in length. Cut three strips of corrugated card, each 7 x 1.5 inches (180 x 43 mm).

2. Cut a length of silver paper about a quarter-inch (10 mm) bigger on all sides than the strips of card laid side by side.

3. Apply double-sided tape to the back of the cardboard strips and trim it to fit. Peel off the backing.

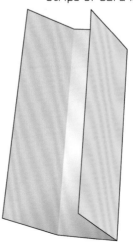

4. Stick the card strips to the back of the silver paper so that they are touching each other. Trim the excess silver paper from around the edges.

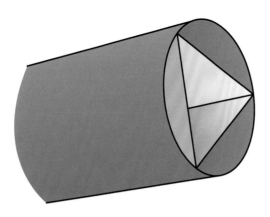

5. Fold along the edges of the card strips and fit the piece into the tube.

6. Pop out one of the lenses from the reading glasses. Cut a circle of cardboard to cover the end of the poster tube and cut a circular hole in the center. to match the width of the lens.

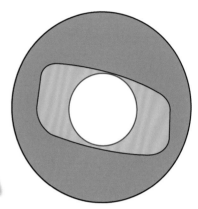

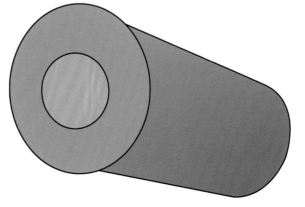

7. Tape the lens in place, making sure not to get tape over the hole.

8. With the lens on the inside, glue the lens holder to the end of the poster tube to complete your kaleidoscope.

9. Point the open end of the kaleidoscope at colorful objects, such as flowers or bright pictures.

Marvel as the reflected colors swirl around when you move the kaleidoscope!

Amazing Science

The kaleidoscope was invented by English scientist Sir David Brewster in 1814. It uses three mirrors set at a slight angle to reflect each other in a perfectly symmetrical (matching) pattern. Colors swirl in different patterns you view objects the lens.

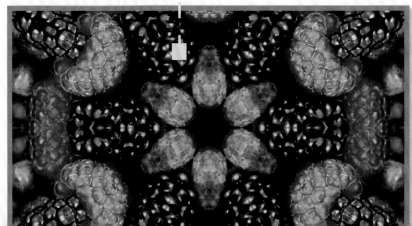

Heliograph

You will need:

The sun

A small pocket mirror x2

A copy of Morse code

In the past, the heliograph was used to communicate over long distances. By flashing sunlight from one person to another, complicated messages could be sent at the speed of light. There are just a few problems with this: it has to be sunny, you must be able to see the person you are sending a message to, and it is s-l-o-w! But you can send a message several miles, and it is very difficult for anyone to eavesdrop.

Try it with a friend using Morse code (below): short flashes for dots and long flashes for dashes.

Line up your friend with a target, and your signal will travel on to reach them too.

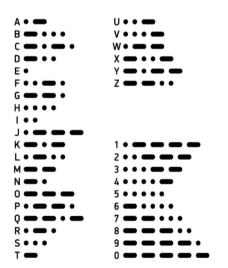

```
A • ▄         U • • ▄
B ▄ • • •      V • • • ▄
C ▄ • ▄ •      W • ▄ ▄
D ▄ • •       X ▄ • • ▄
E •           Y ▄ • ▄ ▄
F • • ▄ •      Z ▄ ▄ • •
G ▄ ▄ •
H • • • •
I • •
J • ▄ ▄ ▄
K ▄ • ▄       1 • ▄ ▄ ▄ ▄
L • ▄ • •      2 • • ▄ ▄ ▄
M ▄ ▄         3 • • • ▄ ▄
N ▄ •         4 • • • • ▄
O ▄ ▄ ▄       5 • • • • •
P • ▄ ▄ •      6 ▄ • • • •
Q ▄ ▄ • ▄      7 ▄ ▄ • • •
R • ▄ •       8 ▄ ▄ ▄ • •
S • • •       9 ▄ ▄ ▄ ▄ •
T ▄           0 ▄ ▄ ▄ ▄ ▄
```

1. Choose an open space with the sun to one side of you when you face each other. Stand on either side of an object and line up your friend with the object.

2. Reflect the sunlight with your mirror onto the ground near you. You should see a bright spot the same shape as your mirror. Now shine it at the object.

3. Move it up just slightly to flash a beam at your friend. It will reach them, because light travels in straight lines.

Ice Lens

You will need:

Dried moss, bark, twigs, or leaves for tinder

Boiled water

Deep bowl with a curved base

Can you start a campfire using just ice? You can if the sun is shining!

1. When the boiled water is cool, pour it into the bowl to a depth of around 2 inches (5 cm). Freeze it overnight to make your ice lens.

Do not place fingers, clothing, or any other materials near the flame. Extinguish the flame immediately upon completing the experiment.

2. Warm the outside of the bowl in warm water and turn the lens out of the bowl into a gloved hand.

3. Arrange your tinder in a fire pit. Use the ice lens to focus the sun's rays on the tinder until it starts to smolder. Arrange some small twigs on top and make yourself a small campfire!

Amazing Science

A convex (outward-bulging) piece of clear ice acts like a lens to focus the sun's rays together. The concentration of light can heat tinder enough to start a fire. Be sure to put out your mini campfire properly afterward!

Microscope

Microscopes reveal a hidden world that you can't see with the naked eye. This super simple microscope lets you magnify 10–20 times—and all it needs is a drop of water! Dutchman Antonie van Leeuwenhoek invented the microscope in the 1660s and discovered all kinds of minute things— from the hairs on a flea to tiny life-forms in pond water.

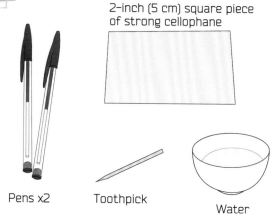

Pens x2

Toothpick

2-inch (5 cm) square piece of strong cellophane

Water

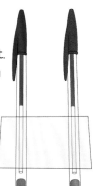

1. Space out two pens roughly 1 inch (3 cm) apart. Balance the cellophane on top as shown.

2. Dip the toothpick in water and transfer a drop to the middle of the cellophane. Keep adding drops of water until the drop on the cellophane is about ¼-inch (5 mm) across. That's your microscope!

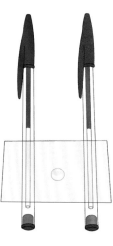

3. You can experiment with different drop sizes. Smaller drops give greater magnification but a narrower field of view. Larger drops give less magnification but a better field of view.

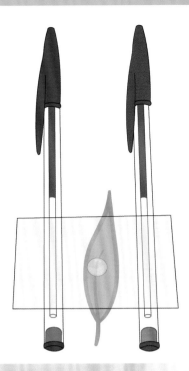

4. Place the object you wish to investigate under the water drop. Look down through the drop to observe the magnified image.

Once you start investigating the microscopic world, there are all sorts of amazing things to see. Try looking at sugar and salt crystals. Can you learn to identify which is which just by its appearance? See if you can persuade an insect to crawl under your microscope. Don't forget to let it go when you have finished your investigation.

See what microscopic discoveries you can make!

Amazing Science

Van Leeuwenhoek discovered mini beasts, such as amoebas (right), with a microscope that was just a tiny bead of glass. Your simple microscope allows you to see tiny things magnified with just a drop of water. The curved surface of the drop acts as the magnification lens.

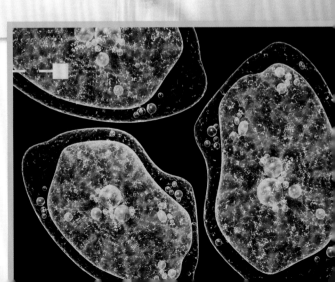

Persistent Pencil

You will need:

Two discs of thin white cardstock, 1.2-inches (30 mm) across

Pencil

Persistence of vision (*see below*) is at the heart of many optical effects and illusions. Here, this effect makes two pictures appear as a single, merged picture.

Tools you will need: (see page 7)

✶ Epoxy glue

1. On one disc, draw a small fish in the center. On the second disc, draw a fishbowl.

2. Glue the two discs back to back, with the pencil sandwiched between them as shown.

3. Spin the pencil briskly between the palms of your hands and watch the fish appear inside the fishbowl.

Amazing Science

When we look at something, the picture stays in our eyes for a moment. This is called persistence of vision. Our brains also fill in the gaps when something moves. These two effects make us see a movie as continuous motion— though it is really a series of rapidly changing still pictures.

Hose Rainbow

Conditions need to be just right for a rainbow to form. There must be sunshine as well as rain, and everything has to line up. The sun has to shine from behind you with the rain in front of you. When this happens, you will see a glorious rainbow!

1. Stand with your back to the sun and set your garden hose to a fine spray. Spray it away from yourself. A rainbow will appear in front of you!

2. Try different settings on the hose attachment to see which makes the best rainbow.

Amazing Science

Rainbows occur when sunlight is reflected within raindrops. The light is split into its colors as it is refracted (bent) by the water. The colors separate because each is bent by a different amount.

21

Spinner

This spinner is an experiment in color mixing! As the disc spins fast, all the colors blur into one, revealing the average color.

You will need:

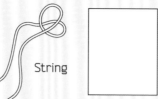

String

Paper

Corrugated cardboard

Colored cardstock

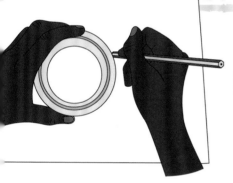

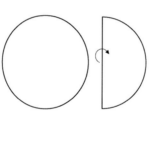

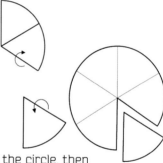

1. Trace the shape of the tape roll onto the paper. Cut out the circle, then fold it into sixths. Cut out one of the six segments. This will be your template.

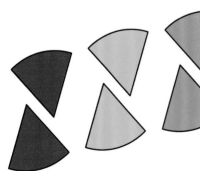

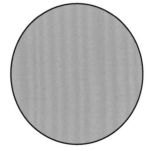

2. Cut out six segments of colored card using your template as a guide.

3. Cut out a corrugated card disc using the same roll of tape as a template.

4. Glue the six segments onto the card as shown.

5. Make two holes off-center on the disc, and thread 30 inches (76 cm) of string through. Spin the disc by winding it up, then rhythmically pulling and releasing to speed it up.

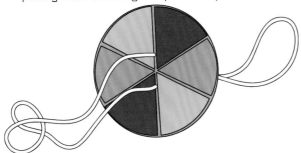

See if you can guess what color you will see before you start spinning. What happens if you mix yellow and red, black and white, blue and red? Are the color mixes the same as when you mix paint? What happens if you only add one slice of one color and five of another? What if you cover the disk in random circles of different colors!?

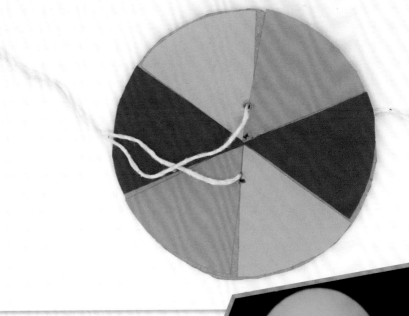

Amazing Science

When you spin a disc of colors, your eyes mix them together. If you combine just three basic, or primary, colors of light (red, blue, and green) you get white. But colored card is not the same as colored light, so here you end up with a brown color!

Stereoscopic Pictures

When you look at an object, you get two slightly different views of it, one to each eye. Your brain merges the picture together to reveal it in 3D! You can also fool your brain by recreating two different views in photographs. These paired pictures can be seen in 3D with the viewer from p. 26.

You Will need:

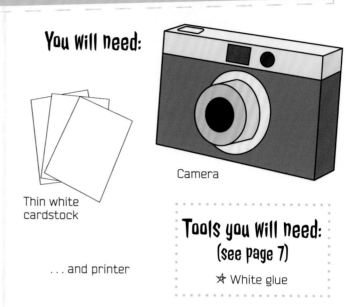

Camera

Thin white cardstock

. . . and printer

Tools you Will need:
(see page 7)
✶ White glue

1. For your pictures, choose a subject with good front-to-back depth. Complex, intricate objects, such as bushes or trees, also work well. Check that the lighting is constant and the object is stationary.

2. Take a photograph. Move 2–2.5 inches (6–7 cm) to your right without turning and take another photograph. These will be your stereo pair.

24

3. Print out both pictures so that they are roughly 2 inches (55 mm) wide. This is the best fit for the viewer in the next project.

4. Glue both pictures to a piece of card with a very small gap between them. The first picture goes on the left, the second on the right.

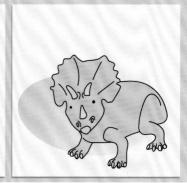

Try other subjects, such as still lifes or outdoor plants . . .

StereoViewer

Corrugated cardboard

A simple viewer allows you to see the 3D effect of the stereoscopic pictures you made on p. 25.

Tools you will need:
(see page 7)

✴ Utility knife
✴ Gaffer tape (or duct tape)
✴ White glue
✴ Clothespins

Strong reading glasses, +3 strength

1. Carefully pop the lenses out of the reading glasses.

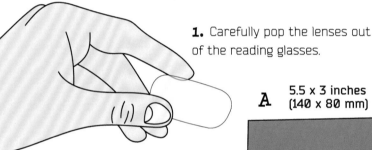

A 5.5 x 3 inches (140 x 80 mm)

C 7.75 x 1.5 inches (200 x 40 mm)

2. Cut out the three pieces A, B, and C as shown. Cut holes in B slightly smaller than the lenses, with the centers 3 inches (80 mm) apart. On C, mark and score tab and center lines. Make notches and fold along the score lines.

B

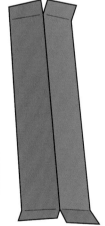

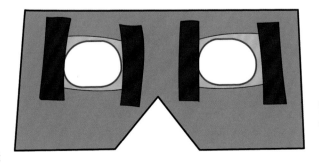

3. Tape the lenses in position with gaffer tape (or duct tape).

4. Assemble the three parts, fixing the tabs with white glue. Use clothespins to hold them together until the glue has dried.

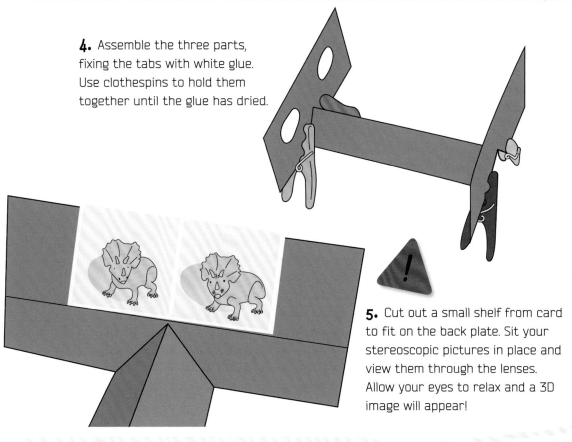

5. Cut out a small shelf from card to fit on the back plate. Sit your stereoscopic pictures in place and view them through the lenses. Allow your eyes to relax and a 3D image will appear!

Amazing Science

The small distance between your eyes means each eye receives a slightly different view of the world. These two different views are transmitted to the brain, which merges them to give the impression of depth and solidity.

Telescope

Pencil

White cardstock

Corrugated cardboard

Two magnifying glasses: one with a wide lens (e.g. 4 inches/75 mm) at 4x magnification; and one with a small lens (e.g. 1 inch/30 mm) at 20x magnification

A single lens can magnify things close by. A telescope allows you to see far away, because it has at least two lenses, or curved mirrors. Dutchman Hans Lippershey, who made magnifiers, is the likely inventor of the telescope in 1608.

Tools you Will need (see page 7)

✯ White glue
✯ Gaffer tape (or duct tape)
✯ Ruler
✯ Utility knife

A poster tube roughly the same diameter as the large lens

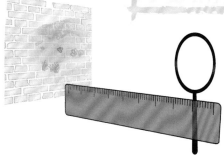

1. Find the focal length of the two lenses. Hold the weaker lens up to focus a clear image from outside onto your wall. Measure the distance from the lens to the wall.

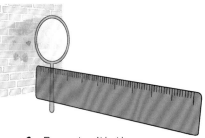

2. Repeat with the more powerful lens. The focal length will be much shorter.

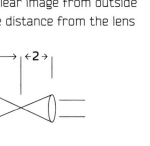

← 16 → ←2→

3. Add the two focal lengths together (example above: 16 cm + 2 cm = 18 cm). Your poster tube should be a couple of centimeters or about a half inch shorter than the combined focal length.

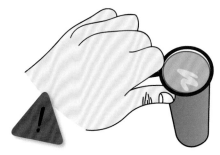

4. Fit the large lens to the end of the poster tube with glue or tape.

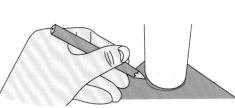

5. Roll up an 8-inch (20 cm) piece of thin white card so that it will just fit inside the tube. Draw around the end on a piece of corrugated cardboard.

6. Cut out the card circle. Cut out a hole in the center and tape the smaller lens over the hole.

7. Fit the inner tube into the outer tube.

8. Tape or glue the small lens over the end of the inner tube. This tube should be able to move back and forwards in the outer tube. Do this to focus your image. Close objects will need a longer tube. Distant objects will need a shorter tube.

9. Look through your telescope. Notice that the image is inverted! This is always the case with this type of telescope.

Don't look at the sun!

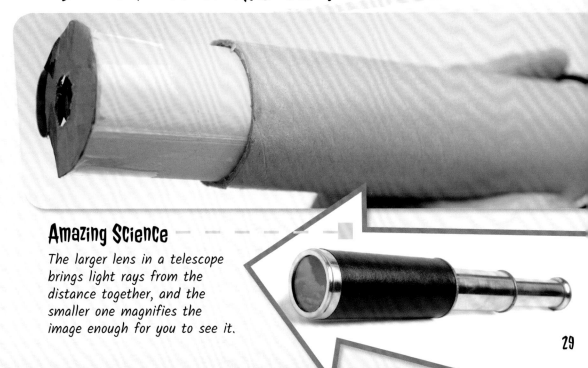

Amazing Science

The larger lens in a telescope brings light rays from the distance together, and the smaller one magnifies the image enough for you to see it.

Glossary

camera obscura: Named after the Latin for dark (obscura) room (camera), it was just that: a dark room with a small hole in one wall. When light from a scene outside beamed through the hole, it produced an upside-down, mirror image of that scene on the opposite wall. Box-like devices were made that mimicked this effect, with a lens inserted into the hole. Artists used these to help them draw and paint scenes accurately. The camera obscura also developed into the box camera that captured images on photosensitive paper.

convex: Curving outwards. (The opposite is concave, or curving inwards.) A convex lens is thicker in the middle than at the edge. Light rays passing through it converge, or are brought close together.

focus: The point were converging light rays meet

lens: A shaped piece of polished glass or plastic used to bend light rays together and focus them or disperse them (spread them out)

persistence of vision: The optical illusion where many short flashing images are merged into a single image by the brain

photon: The basic particle of visible light. Light energy is formed from photons streaming through space at 186,282 miles (299,792 km) per second.

refraction: The bending of light rays, which happens when they move from air into a transparent substance, such as water or glass

stereovision: Also known as 3D vision, the impression of looking at something in 3D. Our two eyes each receive a slightly different picture, and the brain merges them into a single image that has width, height, and depth.

Did You Know?

* The Nimrud lens is the oldest lens, a 3,000-year-old rock crystal discovered in 1850 in what was then Assyria, now Iraq. It may have been used as a magnifying glass or burning glass for starting fires.

Early art from Nimrud, Assyria

* The Hooke Telescope on Mount Wilson in California proved that other galaxies exist and that the universe is expanding.

* The Hubble Space Telescope, launched in 1990, has an 8-ft mirror for collecting available light.

* The earliest microscopes were called flea glasses because they were used for studying insects. An electron microscope can focus on an object one nanometer (one-billionth of a meter) in size and magnify it 5,000,000 times.

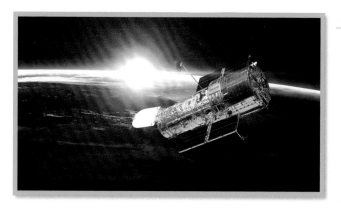

INDEX

The Author

Rob Ives is a former math and science teacher, now a designer and paper engineer living in Cumbria, UK. He creates science- and project-based children's books, including *Paper Models that Rock!* and *Paper Automata.* He specializes in character-based paper animations and all kinds of fun and fascinating science projects, and he often visits schools to talk about design technology and demonstrate his models.

The Illustrator

Eva Sassin is a freelance illustrator born in London, UK. She has always loved illustrating, whether it be scary, fun monsters or cute, sparkly fairies. She carries a sketchbook everywhere, but she has even drawn on the back of receipts if she's forgotten it! In her free time, she travels around London to visit exhibitions and small cafés where she enjoys sketching up new ideas and characters. She is also a massive film buff!